A DICTIONARY OF
MYTHICAL PLACES

A DICTIONARY OF
MYTHICAL PLACES

By *Robin Palmer* · *Illustrated by Richard Cuffari*

HENRY Z. WALCK, INC. · NEW YORK

Text copyright © 1975 by Robin Palmer
Illustrations copyright © 1975 by Richard Cuffari

ISBN: 0-8098-2431-0
LC: 75-6018
Printed in the United States of America

Designed by Aileen Friedman
Library of Congress Cataloging in Publication Data

Palmer, Robin, 1911–
    A dictionary of mythical places.

    SUMMARY: An alphabetically arranged, cross-referenced dictionary of mythical, legendary, and famous literary places briefly describing the origin, location, and major characteristics of each place.
    1. Geographical myths—Juvenile literature.
[1. Geographic myths.   2.   Mythology—Dictionaries]
I.   Cuffari, Richard, 1925–   II.   Title.
GR940.P34   398.2'34   75-6018
ISBN 0-8098-2431-0

Lines from "The Story of a Round-House" reprinted with permission of Macmillan Publishing Co., Inc., from The Story of a Round-House and Other Poems by John Masefield. Copyright 1912, 1913 by Macmillan Publishing Co., Inc., renewed 1940, 1941 by John Masefield.

To Kits, who first introduced me to Camelot and other mythical places.

A DICTIONARY OF
MYTHICAL PLACES

From the earliest times, people have dreamed of places quite different from the lands they lived in—golden cities, magical rivers, or countries where every wish could be fulfilled. Sometimes they imagined islands far out in the mysterious ocean where no ships dared to venture. So persistent were the tales about these places, and so vivid the descriptions, that they were frequently believed to be true. When Christopher Columbus sailed out to find a new route to India, he was also on the lookout for some of these wonderful lands.

But there were other countries where, it was said, human beings could never go. These were the homes of gods and goddesses, or perhaps of monsters and demons. In addition, there have been in all societies many conceptions of the abodes of the dead, whether a paradise or an inferno, and supposedly living beings did occasionally visit some of them.

Besides these legendary places of antiquity, more recent authors have created their own fanciful countries, from Oz to Narnia, which have become famous because of the interesting stories about them. Other writers, not concerned with magic, have tried to imagine an ideal land that human beings might actually construct if laws and government and perhaps the very nature of people were to be changed. Some authors felt they might be able to improve existing social conditions by inventing countries where the things they found wrong with their own were satirized. They hoped that if people were made to laugh at their follies they might want to change to a better way of life.

In addition to these legendary places, the fruit of human imagination, there are a few that may have existed. Some are said to have disappeared beneath the sea. Others, towns or cities, may have been so completely destroyed that no traces of them remain. Archeologists from time to time make discoveries that entirely change our conception of what is legendary and what is real. For years people thought there was nothing historical in the epic tales of Homer, but Heinrich Schliemann was sure that they had a basis of fact, and his excavations uncovering the ancient city of Troy proved that he was right. Many myths probably have hidden truths in them which we do not yet fully understand.

In this book you will find bits of information about all these different types of places—some that never were and some that may have been.

Egyptian

AALU OR AARU

The ancient Egyptians had a firm belief in immortality and a clear conception of Aalu, the land of their departed spirits. It is perhaps an indication of their love for Egypt that they imagined an afterworld to be just like it. As the Nile River was the center of Egyptian life, so the celestial Nile was the center of Aalu. Its deep waters reflected the clear blue of a sunny sky and on either bank were green and fertile fields where the souls of the dead, looking just as they did on earth, tilled the soil, harvested the crops or relaxed on the riverbank. They lived the way they always had, except that they were free from anxiety. The wealthy were buried with "Answerers," small human figures made of clay or stone who came alive and did their master's bidding when it was his turn to sow or reap in the next world.

Greek

ACHERON OR ACHERUSIAN BOG

The Acheron, like the Styx, was one of the legendary rivers surrounding Hades, the Greek underworld. It was a river of woe which the dead must cross on a flat boat, poled by a ferryman. The Greeks thought of it as a dark and polluted stream, but it is also mentioned in medieval Christian legends where its waters are said to be as white as milk. Repentent sinners were cast into it by the archangel Michael and then, having been cleansed by the immersion, they were led to the City of God.

ADLIVUN

Under the sea and ice, the Eskimos believe, there is a world of discomfort where those who have been evildoers on earth receive punishment. It is ruled over by Queen Sedna. She lives in a great house there and owns a huge dog who usually lies across the threshold. Sedna passes judgment on the souls coming into her care, and varies the severity of her punishments according to the wrongs or crimes they have committed. Some souls move on to a more remote place called *Adliparmiut* where life is less disagreeable. There hunters are free to hunt and everyone is at peace, but it is a stormy land of snow and ice, by no means a paradise. It is also a place of no return, either to earth or to a happier existence.

AEAEA

Greek

This mythical island is famous because it was the abode of the beautiful enchantress, Circe. She had the power of changing anyone who visited her shores into whatever beast or bird she fancied. When the Greek hero Odysseus stopped at Aeaea he had no idea where he was, so he climbed a craggy hill close to the shore. From the top he could see all of the small island. In the center were thick woods, and although there was no sign of man or beast, a wisp of smoke rising from among the trees suggested that there must be some sort of dwelling there. Odysseus sent some of his followers to explore, and as they entered the woods they came upon wild beasts, wolves and lions as tame as dogs. When they advanced further they saw a palace built of polished stone. There Circe received them with charming courtesy, gave them food and drink, and promptly transformed them into pigs. But one man, more cautious than the rest, had hidden outside to see what would happen to his companions. He ran back with the news, and Odysseus, protecting himself from enchantment with a sprig of the magic plant, moly, also visited Circe and ultimately persuaded her to restore his followers to their original shapes.

AEOLIAN ISLE

Greek

The Greek myths describe a number of floating islands and one of them was the Aeolian Isle, the home of Aeolus, god of the winds. The island had high, rocky cliffs on every side and these were topped by a strong wall. Aeolus lived in a large palace with his wife, his six sons and six daughters, and all the winds of the world when they were not away doing his bidding. It sounds as if such a floating island might have been blown hither and thither, and it did move about, but Zeus had given Aeolus complete control of the winds so that he was able to subdue the wildest tempest and confine it in a leather bag.

ALBORS OR ALBURZ

Persian

The ancient Persians believed that Albors was a mountain peak around which the sun and moon revolved. Light shone out from the mountain, and on its summit darkness was unknown. There the god Mithras had his dwelling and

AEAEA

from it he could observe what went on all over the world. One legend said that Albors had spreading roots and all the other mountains on earth grew from them.

ALFHEIM

Norse

In the easternmost part of the earth—beside the sacred well of the Norns who are the three Fates of Scandinavian mythology—was Alfheim where the heavenly elves, the alfar, lived. Frey, the sun god, was their king so theirs was a land of light and happiness. The alfar were beautiful little creatures, never misshapen like some of their underground relatives. They were fond of music and dancing and had great supernatural power.

ALTRURIA

William Dean Howells · American

Somewhere, possibly in the Mediterranean Sea, lies the island of Altruria. It was supposed to have been settled by Greeks at the beginning of the Christian era, and Greek culture was combined there with Christian socialism to form an ideal state. Howells introduces Aristides Homos as a traveler from Altruria to America, and has him comment on what he sees: the slums, rural poverty, wasted resources and the labor riots of the 1890's. Homos then describes the ideal conditions in his homeland where some of the same situations had existed and been corrected centuries before. The name of the island is derived from the word "altruism," a chief characteristic of the natives. Howells's articles were published in book form in 1894 under the title *A Traveler from Altruria*.

Japanese   AMA

Ama, the Japanese heaven, has a landscape similar to that of Japan. Across it flows a river with a wide, pebbly bed. This, too, is like the Japanese rivers. Although it is a sky kingdom, Ama is not considered a remote place, and at one time it was thought to have been linked with earth by a bridge, or according to some legends, a staircase, so that the gods and goddesses could go back and forth as they wished. One night, while everyone was asleep, the bridge collapsed and fell into the ocean where it became the beautiful isthmus west of Kyoto.

Hindu   AMARAVATI

Hindu heroes and others who were particularly distinguished for their virtue were transported to Amaravati, a land surrounded by high walls in which there were a thousand gates. None of the anxiety, grief or selfishness of this world was known there. Its orchards continuously bore all kinds of fruits no matter what the season, and all its inhabitants were completely happy. There is actually a ruined city in India called Amaravati which may have been named for the land of bliss.

AMENTI

The Egyptians buried their dead with many things including charms, amulets and weapons to help them make the perilous journey to the other world. Part of the trip was by boat and part over mountains that were inhabited by demons, but the courageous soul, protected by the magic charms, was able to reach Amenti. There the soul was met by the god Anubis, who had the head of a jackal, and was led into an enormous hall for trial. Around the walls of the room sat forty-two judges, some with human and others with animal heads. Osiris, the chief god, had a throne at the far end, and in the center of the floor was a large pair of scales. The soul, looking just like a human being, was required to describe its life on earth, always affirming that it had committed no sin. Then its heart, which was believed to be the seat of the intelligence, was placed on one pan of the scale and the feather of truth on the other. If the two pans balanced perfectly, it proved the soul had spoken the truth. Then it was told by Osiris, whose name means the good one, that all doors were open and it might proceed at once to Aalu, the fields of the blessed. But if the scales failed to balance, the heart was thrown to a monster—part lion, part hippopotamus and part crocodile—and the ravenous creature gobbled it up and with it the immortality of the soul.

ANNUVIN, ANNWFN OR ANNWN

Celtic

In Welsh folklore, especially in the *Mabinogian*, we have some glimpses of this land whose name literally translated means "not the world." Some said it was located in the far north and ruled over by King Arawn. Others have placed it under or over the sea. But everyone agrees that it was a country of great beauty and delight, a wild land of rugged mountains and rushing streams. Those who lived there were skilled in magic and possessed most unusual animals. They also possessed a marvelous cauldron that could produce any number of hot meals. As long as the inhabitants were brave, they never went hungry; but the cauldron could sense the presence of a coward and would refuse to provide any food. Annuvin was a land of great treasures, not only magic ones but also gold, precious stones and works of art. Consequently people raided it in order to steal whatever they could, and in spite of the fact that they lived in a land of plenty, the inhabitants of Annuvin also made raids on our world. They were accompanied by a pack of white hounds with red ears.

Portuguese

ANTILIA

Antilia, which was sometimes called the Island of the Seven Cities, was somewhere in the Atlantic Ocean, but it could be visited only by chance. No one who looked for it could ever find it. A group of sailors claimed that their ship had gone aground there, and although they were the first to describe it, they were never able to return. They said that the seven cities had been settled by seven bishops and their followers who had been driven from the Iberian peninsula by the Moors. Upon their arrival in Antilia they burned their boats so that no one could leave, but before long no one wanted to leave. The entire population was happy and prosperous. They were also very religious, due

AMENTI

to the continuous efforts of the bishops. The sailors attributed the Antilians' prosperity to the fact that there was much gold on the island. It was said to glitter in the sands of the beaches. When Columbus named the Antilles he was undoubtedly thinking, perhaps hopefully, of this fabulous island.

APSU OR ABSU   *Babylonian*

The Apsu was an abyss filled with fresh water. In the center of it lay the earth, like a floating island which was believed to be almost circular and fairly flat. On the borders of this island earth were high mountain ranges, tall enough to hold up the sky. Where the Apsu's waters burst through the earth's surface there were springs, lakes and rivers. This concept was among the most primitive in Babylonian mythology.

ARALU OR ARALLU   *Babylonian*

Some Babylonian myths described the vast underworld city of Aralu, an abode of the dead. It was like an enormous cavern just beneath the earth's surface. The inhabitants had the form of winged shadows and led a dreary existence, though they could sometimes return to earth in search of food and drink.

ARCADIA, ARCADY   *Greek*

A mountainous district in southern Greece has been idealized in stories and poems as the dwelling place of Pan, the god of pastures and forests as well as flocks and herds. It is a place where people are always happy, contented with simple rustic pastimes, where shepherds play their flutes while shepherdesses dance. One or two ancient authors described the Arcadians as simpletons.

Persian

ARDVISURA ANAHITA

High up in the air, according to Persian mythology, is a milk-filled lake known as Ardvisura Anahita. Beside it and spreading its branches over it, is the great tree of life. From the lake flow four celestial rivers, one for each main point of the compass.

Teutonic

ASGARD

The vast country where the gods and goddesses of Teutonic mythology had their dwellings was called Asgard. It was a place of great natural beauty with farmlands and orchards, hills and valleys, and it was divided into twelve realms, each the home of a particular god who ruled over it. It was connected with the earth by a wide rainbow bridge called Bifrost. The gods could gallop over the rainbow on their various steeds—all but Thor. He had to come and go on foot because he was accustomed to riding about in an iron chariot, pulled by huge goats, and it was feared that this thunderous vehicle was heavier than the bridge could bear. No enemy was able to enter Asgard because the bridge was guarded night and day by the god Heimdall. He could see in the dark, and his hearing was so acute that he was aware even of wool growing on the backs of the sheep.

ASTEROID B 612

Antoine de Saint-Exupéry · French

The little prince in Saint-Exupéry's 1943 book of that name came from a planet that was scarcely larger than a house. It had on it three volcanoes—two active ones which were very handy for heating breakfast, and one that was extinct —but of course they were miniature volcanoes. "Where I live," said the little prince, "everything is *so* small." He cleaned out the volcanoes every week so that they would burn gently without violent eruptions. He also cleaned out the one that seemed extinct because with a volcano you can't always be sure it won't erupt again. There was grass on the asteroid and tiny daisylike flowers that bloomed in the morning and faded away at night. There were also baobob trees that had to be uprooted as soon as they began to sprout because they might grow so enormous that their roots would split the planet. But there was one plant the little prince watered and cared for, and that was a beautiful rose, the only rose on Asteroid B 612.

ATLANTIS

Classical

Probably no other land has excited the interest and imagination of so many people as Atlantis. John Masefield has given us his description in *The Story of a Round House.*

In some green island of the sea
  Where now the shadowy coral grows,
In pride and pomp and empery
  The courts of old Atlantis rose.

In many a glittering house of glass
  The Atlanteans wandered there,
The paleness of their faces was
  Like ivory, so pale they were.

Plato, the Greek philosopher, located Atlantis in the ocean west of the Strait of Gibralter. According to his description, said to have originated with ancient Egyptian priests, the island had been a powerful kingdom about the year 9600 B.C. At that time its rulers were supposed to have controlled much of the land bordering on the Mediterranean. Then at the height of Atlantis's power, there was a tremendous earthquake and tidal wave, and the whole island sank beneath the sea.

In another book Plato described Atlantis as an ideal commonwealth with a perfect climate, fertile soil and very happy people. It was a large island divided into ten parts, each of which was ruled by a king, but there was an agreement among them that they should never make war on one another. The capital city, also called Atlantis, was circular. In its center was a high hill where the ten kings met together at a temple of Poseidon, the god of the sea. This temple contained a stone column on which all the laws of the ten kingdoms were inscribed. Below the hill was a fertile plain broken by three circular and concentric streams forming an island within an island. The streams were navigable and connected by canals so that ships could come in to the heart of the city. The bridges were high enough that ships could pass under them without difficulty.

For many years people have sought Atlantis not only in the Atlantic Ocean where Plato located it, but wherever there are tales of sunken lands, most recently in the Aegean Sea. There it is known that the island of Thera or Santonini had in its center a volcano surrounded by a fertile plain where people lived in an advanced state of civilization. In about 1450 B.C. the volcano erupted with such violence that the island virtually blew up. The disturbance must have been great enough to send tidal

ATLANTIS

waves over the shores of Greece, Asia Minor and Crete. The coast of Thera, where cities had once stood, disappeared beneath the sea. This discovery does not agree with Plato's description either in date or location, but many people have thought Plato might have been inaccurate since he admits his information to have been third hand. Others have thought that Plato invented Atlantis in order to describe some of his utopian ideas.

AVALON   *Celtic*

Avalon was the island home of the fairy queen Morgan le Fay and her numerous sisters. It was a pleasant land with apple orchards and beautiful gardens where plants of every description flourished. Here was forged the sword King Arthur used in his early battles, and it was to Avalon that three fairy queens bore him when he was mortally wounded. Morgan le Fay was said to have magic powers of healing which she used to bring about King Arthur's complete recovery, so he has been living in Avalon ever since, awaiting the time for his return to Britain.

In the thirteenth century two graves were discovered in Glastonbury Abbey, and they were supposedly marked with the names of Arthur and his queen. These graves are still pointed out to tourists who visit the ruins. As a result of this discovery, some people began to call the vale of Glastonbury Avalon, but that was certainly not the place indicated in the original legend. There had long been tales of a Celtic island of fairy women where a hero might live forever.

SEE HADES AVERNUS

Aztec   AZTLAN

Aztec legends claim that their people originated on an island known as Aztlan. It was a bright land of shining light and whiteness which contained seven cities surrounding a sacred mountain. In the mountain were seven caves out of which came the seven tribes of Iztac Mixcoatl. No one has ever located this island and it is generally believed to be mythical, though there are people who associate it with Atlantis which was said to have distant colonies.

The name Aztlan has also been used in a poem by Robert Southey. It tells about a Welsh hero, Prince Madoc, the youngest son of Owen Gwynnedd who lived in the twelfth century. Despite his royal rank, Madoc was a brave sailor and fisherman. One day, distressed by a war between his father and his brothers, he set sail into the unknown Atlantic and founded a settlement far off in the west. All this is part of Welsh tradition. As Southey describes it, the settlement was called Aztlan, and the prince once returned to Wales to encourage more settlers to go out with him to the fruitful country he had discovered.

SEE GULLIVER'S TRAVELS BALNIBARBI

Miguel de Cervantes · Spanish   BARATARIA

In *Don Quixote de la Mancha* (1605, 1615) the knight's squire, Sancho Panza, though an ignorant peasant, becomes ambitious to be the governor of an island realm. When the duke hears about it, he thinks it would be amusing to appoint Sancho governor of Barataria, a small place with a population of only a thousand and not an island at all. Sancho gladly accepts the position together with the fine clothes and the palace suitable to his new rank. He has no sooner arrived, however, when tricks are played on him which he has not the wit to understand. At dinner delicious platters of food are placed before him but his steward orders them taken away for fear they might be poisoned, and the poor governor is allowed hardly anything to eat. Finally Sancho is told that enemies are invading his territory. Much against his will he is clapped into some ill-fitting armor, and although he can hardly move or see, he is able to hear loud noises that he is sure are sounds of battle. The confusion terrifies him and he decides he was never cut out to be a governor. All he wants is to mount his old donkey and go home to his wife.

In the comic opera *The Gondoliers*, written over two centuries after *Don Quixote*, W. S. Gilbert borrows the name Barataria for his country where two gondoliers are ruling jointly while waiting to find out which one is king. They complain that they are being given only enough food for one person. Barataria is derived from the Spanish word for cheap.

BENSALEM   *Francis Bacon · English*

In his book *The New Atlantis* (1626), Bacon describes a journey from Peru to Japan during which his ship is driven off course by a violent gale. After many days, when some of the sailors have become ill and the food has nearly given out, the captain is relieved to see an island in the distance. This turns out to be Bensalem. As the ship nears shore, a small boat comes out to meet it, and the captain is given a scroll written in ancient Hebrew, Greek and Latin—one of which travelers of old would surely understand. It states that if repairs are needed, the ship may lie at anchor for sixteen days. When the inhabitants learn about the sick crew members, however, they permit everyone to come ashore and stay in their strangers' hall where they are well fed and treated with great kindness and courtesy. Only one of their number is allowed to leave the building and wander about the island.

He is amazed to find that these remote islanders know about all the other continents and are aware of recent inventions and discoveries. The governor explains that Bensalem had an academy of wise men, known as the Society of Solomon's House, and certain members are always traveling and returning home to tell what they have learned. In this way the islanders keep abreast of science and the arts as well as changes in government in the rest of the world. From this information as well as constant study and experiment at home, they are able to maintain the best possible conditions for all their people. Of the few outsiders who have been permitted to visit Bensalem, most have been invited to stay permanently. The others, on reaching their homes, describe the island as such an ideal place that no one believes in its existence.

John Bunyan · English   BEULAH LAND

In *The Pilgrim's Progress*, published in 1678, Bunyan describes the journey of a man called Christian to the

Celestial City. After he has passed the territory of the Giant Despair, he and his companions linger in Beulah Land which is beyond the Valley of the Shadow of Death. It is a land of perpetual spring and a place of peace and quiet, where they can listen every day to the singing of birds and enjoy watching flowers come into bloom. It is also within sight of the Celestial City.

BIG ROCK CANDY MOUNTAIN

American

This is the happy land of tramps and hoboes described in song. Anything the tramp fears is rendered harmless. The dogs have rubber teeth, the police have wooden legs, and all the jails are made of tin.

BIMINI

Spanish

Somewhere in the neighborhood of the Bahamas there is a legendary island on which the fountain of youth may be found. A drink from its waters will not only restore youth, but also give immortality. Ponce de Leon, the Spanish explorer, was so excited by the prospect that he set out to find it, searching not only the islands but even the mainland of Florida. There is a real pair of islands bearing this name, but lacking the fountain.

BLEFUSCU SEE GULLIVER'S TRAVELS

Procopius · Byzantine   BRITTIA

In the fifth century A.D. the Byzantine lawyer and historian Procopius wrote a description of the island of Brittia. He said that it was divided in two parts by a wall that ran from north to south, but only the eastern part could be inhabited because the air in the west was so polluted that only snakes and evil creatures could survive there. Brittia was not a land of the dead, and yet the invisible spirits of those who had died in Europe were ferried there by fishermen. This was the first stage of their journey to the other world. The fishermen, who were natives of Brittia, said that they could hear their ghostly passengers talking, answering the questions of another invisible being who met them. Some scholars believe that Procopius was giving a very confused description of Britain, and that the wall he mentioned was the Roman wall.

SEE GULLIVER'S TRAVELS   BROBDINGNAG

Celtic   BROCELIANDE

Tennyson in *Idylls of the King* (1859–1885) tells us that

> *in the wild woods of Broceliande,*
> *Before an oak so hollow, huge and old*
> *It looked a tower of ivied masonwork,*
> *At Merlin's feet the wily Vivien lay.*

Vivien, a beautiful but malicious maiden, was determined to accomplish the downfall of King Arthur by killing or

BROCELIANDE

capturing the aged enchanter, Merlin. She pretended to be in love with the old man and went with him to the shores of Brittany. From there she followed him on foot to the legendary forest of Broceliande where she finally persuaded him to teach her some of his magic charms. When a wild storm arose and he crept into a hollow oak for shelter, she bewitched him so that he fell asleep and then imprisoned his body forever in the tree.

CAER SIDI   *Celtic*

Some ancient legends of Wales describe an otherworld called Caer Sidi, which means revolving castle. It is a huge structure with many towers and massive glass walls from the top of which silent archers watch for possible intruders. The castle never ceases to revolve as if its foundations were a turntable, and since it has only one narrow door in its sloping, glass wall, it would be hard enough to enter even if one could elude the archers. Though no light shows from outside, the inside of the castle is said to be brightly illuminated, and much feasting and revelry goes on there. Among the many treasures of Caer Sidi is a pearl-rimmed cauldron from which nine pythonesses, who may be priestesses of the druids, derive their prophesies.

CAMELOT   *Celtic*

Camelot is the name of the ancient city where King Arthur held his court. It was built on a mountain in the midst of a broad plain—a beautiful, walled city whose spires and turrets tended to appear and disappear in the frequent mists, making it seem to be part of fairyland. Its gates were magnificently carved with dragons and the figures of the three fairy queens who were friends to Arthur. For centuries people have tried to locate the site of the city, and there are those who claim to have been successful. Some have placed it in Cornwall, where we still find the Camel River and the ruins of Tintagel Castle. Others have located it at Caerleon in the Welsh county of Monmouthshire where archeologists have uncovered an amphitheater and a fortress probably used by the Romans in the first century. Malory—who wrote about Arthur in the fifteenth century, nearly a thousand years after the king is thought to have lived—said that Camelot was at Winchester and it is there that tourists are shown the huge tabletop that is supposed to be the original round table.

Aztec

CATCITEPULZ

This is the name of a talking mountain in Aztec mythology. It summoned people to come to it and do penance for their sins.

Jewish

CHELM

The legendary town of Chelm looks like many another. It has a main street, a town hall, shops and houses. It even has one skyscraper where its wise men go to solve the problems of the community. All the people of Chelm are foolish but they have great faith in their wise men, so much so that if the wise men are high in the skyscraper trying to think something through, the people in the street below speak only in whispers. It is well-known that the slightest sound will disturb the thought processes. But the wise men's solutions seem rather surprising. For example, the people asked them what to do about a dangerous road. It passed so close to the edge of a cliff that travelers had fallen off and been seriously hurt. The wise men thought and thought. Then they solved the problem. They had a hospital built at the foot of the cliff.

There actually is a town in Poland called Chelm, but the people there are quite normal.

CLOUD-CUCKOO-LAND   see NEPHELOCOCCYGIA

COCKAIGNE or COCKAYNE

French and British

It is interesting how many mythical places have been conceived where delicious food may be had for the asking. Cockaigne was famous in medieval song and story. Perhaps the first description of it was in a French poem of the thirteenth century. It was the land of cakes. Some of the houses were made of barley sugar and the streets were paved with pastry. But if a visitor lacked a sweet tooth, there was a huge kettle on a mountain of cheese. It was overflowing with hot macaroni and dumplings that frequently rolled down the hill, picking up a coating of cheese on the way. There were even roast pigs running about the streets with a knife and fork stuck in their backs. Far from suffering, they were almost asking to be eaten before the air cooled them off too much.

SEE SYMPLEGADES CYANEAN ROCKS

John Bunyan · English DELECTABLE MOUNTAINS

The pilgrims in Bunyan's *Pilgrim's Progress* (1678) finally reached the Delectable Mountains where they found gardens, orchards and vineyards. They also came upon a fountain of clear, fresh water where they could wash off the dust of their journey. On top of the mountains sheep were grazing, and the four shepherds who were camping nearby said that their master had told them to give food and shelter to strangers. The pilgrims spent the night in their tents and in the morning the shepherds took them for a walk. They pointed out various landmarks—Doubting Castle, which was owned by a giant named Despair, the Country of Conceit, and other places the pilgrims should avoid. Then they showed them the way to their destination and hastened them on their journey.

Greek DELOS

The island of Delos is legendary only in its origin. It was said to be one of several floating islands described in classical mythology, and it was finally chained in place as a

COCKAIGNE

reward for giving a home to Leto. She was a young Titon who was loved by Zeus and consequently hated by his wife, Hera. She wandered many miles seeking shelter, but no land was willing to accept her because of Hera's hostility. At last she saw a tiny, barren island floating on the sea. It was pushed about by the wind and when it bumped against the shore, Leto managed to scramble onto its rocky surface. This was Delos, and when she asked permission to stay there, it welcomed her gladly. One version of the myth says that four huge pillars of stone grew up from the bottom of the sea and supported the island, but whether it was held by chains or pillars, the result was that it never moved again. It was there that the twins Artemis and Apollo were born.

DILMUN   *Sumerian*

The ancient Sumerians had a myth which described Dilmun as a holy land, a place where there was no sickness or death, and where everything was clean and bright. According to the myth, there was no fresh water in Dilmun until the god Enki ordered the sun god Uti to provide water that was pure and crystal-clear. This turned the land into a garden with green fields, meadows, flowers and fruit trees. It has been compared with the Garden of Eden and, though it was a paradise of the gods, one man is said to have lived there, a survivor of the great deluge. This was Utu-nipishtim, the Sumerian Noah.

In recent times, as more and more of the ancient tablets have been unearthed and translated, references to Dilmun as a real place and an important trading center have been found. Archeologists believe they have located it on the island of Bahrain in the Persian Gulf near the Arabian coast. Its history goes back more than 4,500 years.

Hebrew   EDEN

According to the biblical story in Genesis, the Garden of Eden was the place where the first man and woman, Adam and Eve, were created and made their home. They were driven out because of their disobedience. It was a beautiful garden with luxuriant flowers and trees. A river flowed through it and from this river ran four streams, two of which were the Tigris and the Euphrates. The other two streams were also named in the biblical account. They were the Pishon, a river that was said to encircle a land of gold and carnelians, and the Gihon. Neither of these can be identified today.

During the middle ages and for some time afterward, there was a great deal of interest in finding Eden. It was thought to have remained just as beautiful as it had been in the days of Adam and Eve. Sir John Mandeville, a rather unreliable author of the fourteenth century, claimed that he had located it and described the place although he admitted that he had never been there. He said it was the highest spot in the world, so high that it was very near the sun. Around it was a wall covered with moss, but there was no gate. Outside the wall and completely surrounding the garden was a ring of blazing fire to discourage anyone from trying to enter. In addition, vicious beasts roamed the area. Mandeville said that all the fresh waters of the world flowed from the center of Eden. They ran underground to spring up in various places such as Egypt, where they formed the Nile, and India, where they became the Ganges.

EL DORADO *Spanish*

El Dorado was the name of a legendary king who was thought to rule over a city of immense wealth. Some people believed the city was on the Amazon River and others located it on the Orinoco, but none of the Spanish and English explorers who searched for it met with any success. The king was said to have such a love for gold that he had his body coated with oil and then heavily powdered with gold dust. As time passed, the name of the king was given to the city where he lived, and later to the country where it was located. Now El Dorado is used to refer to any region, real or legendary, where gold and precious stones abound.

In 1759 Voltaire published *Candide,* in which he tells what he thinks El Dorado must be like. Candide and his valet arrive there by chance when their small boat is caught in rapids and rushed into an underground watercourse beneath the Andes. The first thing they notice when they emerge is that the children alongside the river are playing with toys made of gold and jewels. When they are called to school, they casually drop their playthings as if they have no value. The two men are well received in El Dorado and even entertained by the king. Far from loving gold, the king and his subjects have little interest in it. The people have everything they need and they all live in perfect harmony. Candide is also impressed by the fact that large red sheep are used instead of horses, and when he desires to leave the country, he is presented with a number of these sheep, laden with gold and precious stones.

see FAIRYLAND ELFLAND

ELYSIAN FIELDS, ELYSIUM OR FORTUNATE FIELDS

Classical

The earliest Greek conception of Paradise was known as the Elysian Fields. It was described as a delightful place where those who had led virtuous lives on earth found complete contentment. Some enjoyed games and sports; others had horses and dogs with them, and still others played the lyre. It was located at the ends of the earth and ruled by Rhadamanthys, a son of Zeus, who was known for his integrity and fairness. Much later poets, such as Virgil, located the Elysian Fields next to the gloomy underworld of Hades, but wherever its location might be, Elysium was always a land of light and happiness.

EMPYREAN

Classical

In ancient times the universe was conceived by many as a layered structure having an underworld, our earth, and the heavens which also had various tiers. The highest level of all was the empyrean, the source of all light. It was a place too brilliant for mortal eyes, and there were those who believed it to be composed of pure fire.

see MAILDUN'S VOYAGE ENCOS

Erewhon is very nearly nowhere-spelled-backwards. In Samuel Butler's book, published in 1872, it was a country supposedly discovered by an Englishman named Higgs who had been working on a sheep farm in a remote part of the globe. Mr. Higgs felt that the snowy ranges behind the farm might contain gold, so he set out to explore the region. High in the mountains, when he was already uneasy because of the solitude, he heard a sort of unearthly music that he later discovered came from a circle of enormous and hideous human figures made of stone. Their heads were hollow so the wind blowing through them made an eerie tune. This prehistoric circle marked the entrance to Erewhon.

When Higgs proceeded further he met some of the people of the land, beautiful women and handsome men, all with dark hair. He later discovered that the Erewhonian ideal was good looks, good health and a good bank balance. Illness was punished by imprisonment, but a tendency to commit crimes was considered a misfortune to be cured. Therefore criminals were not locked up but visited at home by a person called a straightener, because they obviously needed straightening. Treatment might include flogging or a diet restricted to bread and water, but always administered with sympathy.

One of the laws of the land was that no one should own a machine of any kind. The Erewhonians had once had ingenious types of machinery, but all that was left, including clocks and watches, was kept in a museum of antiquities. One of their wise men, some centuries before Higgs's visit, had warned them that if they did not do this machines would become their masters.

The book is a satire. Butler wanted to show how irrational many people are wherever they live.

SEE HOBBITON ERIADOR

ERIDU

Babylonian

There was actually an ancient city in Mesopotamia called Eridu, but the legendary one is described in the tales about Gilgamesh, the Babylonian hero and king of Erech. It was a walled city beside the sea. To reach it, Gilgamesh had to penetrate Mount Mashu whose gates were guarded by scorpion men so huge that their heads touched the terraces of the gods. They allowed Gilgamesh to go through the gates and on through a pitch-dark tunnel in the heart of the mountain. After many hours he saw light ahead and soon entered a magnificent garden. In its center was a tree with branches of lapis lazuli. From each blue twig hung unusual fruit, and the ground beneath the tree was strewn with precious stones. In the garden there was a house belonging to the goddess Siduri Sabitu, and beyond was the sea Gilgamesh was determined to cross in his search for immortality.

FAIRYLAND

European

Fairies come in many shapes and sizes, but the dainty little people who love music and dancing and sometimes have iridescent wings live in Fairyland. It is usually described as an underground kingdom, though in some tales it is said to be at the bottom of a lake or in the heart of a dark forest. The houses and palaces are just like human dwellings in miniature, but there the resemblance to earthly life ceases, for Fairyland is free from ugliness, sickness and worry, and time is nonexistent. The Scottish name for Fairyland is Elfland.

FIDDLERS' GREEN
British

Sailors have imagined their own happy land where fiddles play continuously and the dancers never grow weary. It is a place of merriment where free grog and tobacco are in unlimited supply.

FIELD OF ASPHODEL
Classical

The asphodel of the Mediterranean region is a flower of the lily family, white or pale yellow in color. The ancient Greeks planted it on graves, and associated it with death. In mythology the Field of Asphodel was full of these blossoms, and it was there that the spirits of the dead had to wait until their fates had been decided.

FLATLAND
Edwin Abbott · American

It is difficult for us to imagine a land of only two dimensions, and even more difficult to imagine flat people who slide about their country without any feet, and who think and speak without any apparent heads. They live in flat houses surrounded by flat trees, located on flat streets. Flatland is governed by the Chief Circle and it is a very class-conscious society; the nobility being polygons, the gentlemen, pentagons and the professional people, squares. Soldiers and laborers are triangles, and all the women are straight lines, very sharp and dangerous. If you put a needle on a tabletop and look at it, keeping your eye on a level with the table edge, you will understand something of the limited vision of these people. This naturally results in failure of recognition, and many other complications which seem humorous to us who are too solid to have such problems. Abbott's description of this geometrical country is fascinating. The book, written almost a century ago, is really a forerunner of our science fiction.

GANDERCLEUGH

Scottish

Gandercleugh may be freely translated "folly cliff." It is a place where the people tend to make fools of themselves, in the style of geese—often considered stupid birds. In his book, *Tales of My Landlord,* Sir Walter Scott locates Gandercleugh midway between Edinburgh and Glasgow, where many people traveling by coach or on horseback stop to spend the night.

GARDEN OF MIRTH

Romaunt of the Rose

In an English translation of the French *Le Roman de la Rose,* part of which is said to have been written by Chaucer, we read about the Garden of Mirth. The poet is invited into

FIDDLERS' GREEN

the garden by Idleness, one of the many allegorical persons dwelling there. He meets the gods of Love, Gladness and Courtesy, but also persons representing Shame, Jealousy, Danger and Falseness. In the center of the garden is the Fountain of Narcissus, and reflected in its waters is a perfect rose tree with one particular rosebud so beautiful that the poet falls in love with it. He therefore tries to pick it, and is aided or interfered with by all those in the garden. At last Jealousy protects the rose by building a castle around it. The entire romance is supposed to be the dream of the poet.

GARDEN OF THE HESPERIDES

Greek

When the goddess Hera was married to Zeus, one of her wedding presents was a tree that bore golden apples. Some mythologists have described it as the tree of life. At any rate, it was so precious that it was planted in the Garden of the Hesperides where its fruits could be guarded from thieves. The garden was in a remote part of the west, possibly in northwest Africa. The Hesperides, who were beautiful nymphs, were supposed to guard the apples but since they were hardly powerful enough to contend with violent adversaries, a dragon with a hundred heads was also put in the garden and curled himself around the tree.

GEHENNA SEE SHEOL

GINNUNGAGAP

Teutonic–Scandinavian

In the Teutonic creation myths, there is said to have been an abyss known as Ginnungagap between the fiery region of Muspelheim, the Land of Fire, and the misty dampness of Niflheim. Freezing winds from this fathomless abyss turned the rivers into chunks of ice that made a thundering sound as they fell into the chasm. Sparks from Muspelheim fell on the ice and made steam which turned into layer upon layer of hoarfrost, and this finally became the giant Ymir. Later, when Ymir was slain by the gods Vili and Ve, they threw his body into the abyss and it became the earth.

GIUDECCA

see INFERNO

GJOL

see NIFLHEIM

GLASS MOUNTAIN

European

At the end of the world, in the days when the world was said to be flat with ends where one might be confronted with a falling-off place, there was thought to be a mountain of glass. This mountain is described in the folklore of eastern and central Europe, as well as in that of Britain and Scandinavia. In most of the stories the hero is required to climb it before he can win the hand of the princess. Witches, ogres and swan maidens live in the vicinity, as do eagles, ants, bears and other creatures, and many of them are eager to help the hero in return for some kindness he has done them in the past.

GARDEN OF THE HESPERIDES

GLUBBDUBDRIB SEE GULLIVER'S TRAVELS

GODEU, GODDEU OR   *Celtic*
CAD GODEU In this legendary Welsh forest, the famous battle of the
trees took place. Occasionally in mythology and in some
modern fantasies such as George MacDonald's *Phantastes,*
trees are able to move about. They have gnarled arms and
legs and faces like the trees in some of the old Arthur
Rackham illustrations. Sometimes they are kind and friendly
and sometimes hostile. In the battle of the trees of Godeu,
however, they actually turned into warriors, and the fungi
of the forest turned into horses and dogs. The battle was
between Amarthon, god of the fields and agriculture, and
Arawn, king of the underworld. Perhaps because the trees
took part, Amarthon was victorious.

GONDOR SEE HOBBITON

GOTHAM   *English*

There are several legendary villages said to be populated
by fools, though the natives of Gotham are usually referred
to as the wise men. Supposedly it is an English village, and
there really is a village of that name in England, but some
of the tales about the wise men of Gotham originate as far
away as India. A typical story is about twelve men on a
fishing trip who mourn for one of their number who must
have drowned because each one who counted the group
forgot to count himself.

Dean Swift probably contributed more descriptions of imaginary places to English literature than any other writer. In *Gulliver's Travels*, which was published in 1726, he was satirizing the political and social situation in England, but at the same time he was writing a fascinating tale of travel and adventure. His hero, Lemuel Gulliver, was a ship's surgeon whose first notable voyage ended in shipwreck near the island of LILLIPUT where the tallest man was about six inches high, and all the animals, trees and buildings were in the same proportion. Across a narrow channel from Lilliput was BLEFUSCU, the land of its bitter enemies. Here, too, the inhabitants were tiny. They and the Lilliputians believed there were no countries other than their own in the world. One day, Gulliver fortunately saw an overturned rowboat in the distance and was able to have it hauled ashore by a fleet of little ships. Later he repaired it and used it as a means of escape.

On his next voyage Gulliver was abandoned by some sailors in BROBDINGNAG, where the men were about as tall as one of our church steeples. These giants recognized that he was an intelligent being and taught him their language. They asked him about his homeland and helped him to find out as much as possible about their country. He traveled with the royal family in what they considered a small box, but which to him was a large room with furnishings of a convenient size, and windows through which he could see the countryside.

Brobdingnag was a peninsula with mountains nearly thirty miles high cutting it off from some continent or other. The mountains were impassable so no one knew who might live on the other side. Brobdingnag itself was well populated and had fifty-one cities, about a hundred walled towns and

a large number of villages. All the plants and flowers were on the same gigantic scale as the people, and so were the birds and animals. One morning at the seashore an eagle seized Gulliver's traveling box and carried it far out over the ocean. There he was attacked by several other huge birds and dropped the box which was picked up soon after by an English ship.

In spite of the hazards and misfortunes of his previous journeys, Gulliver set out in 1706 on a third voyage. This time he was captured by pirates and set adrift in a small boat. He had managed to land on a rocky island when he saw overhead what we would describe as a huge flying saucer. Men were fishing from it with long lines. Gulliver waved at them frantically and shouted until they noticed him and lowered a chain with a seat on the end. Then they drew him up to visit the flying city of LAPUTA.

Laputa was a perfectly round city with terraces rising one above the other and connected by staircases. In the center, on the highest level, was the elegant palace of the king. The people of Laputa were a strange race of scientists, philosophers and musicians. Their heads were permanently inclined to the side so that one eye looked up and the other down. Their garments were decorated with stars and musical instruments, and Gulliver later discovered that their minds were so absorbed with theories of mathematics, music and astronomy that they never realized anyone was speaking to them unless they were first alerted by being struck lightly with an inflated bladder. The king invited Gulliver to a fascinating banquet where every course was related to geometry or music. The meat was cut in the shape of triangles and rhomboids, the bread in cones, and the puddings and other dishes molded to look like harps, flutes or drums.

From Laputa Gulliver was lowered to a land under the same domain, the country of BALNIBARBI. He soon noticed that the people in its capital city, Lagado, seemed miserable. They looked unhappy, their houses were run down and their clothes were threadbare. In the countryside things were no better. Farming methods were ineffective and no one seemed to be making any progress. Gulliver learned that this was the direct result of great efforts on the part of learned men to improve the welfare of mankind. Using oldfashioned methods, however satisfactory they may have been, was frowned upon because new and better ones would soon be discovered. Meanwhile everything became dilapidated.

In every town in Balnibarbi was an academy where experiments were being carried on, but were seldom completed. Gulliver visited the laboratory of one scholar who tried endlessly to extract sunbeams from cucumbers, and another who was determined to find a use for spider webs. Perhaps the most interesting experiment involved an enormous machine on which were fastened thousands and thousands of words, each on a separate card. The machine was put in motion and when it came to a stop, people with very little education could copy the groups of words that happened to come together, and so compose poems or books of philosophy. The works they had completed were so remarkably learned that no one in the world could understand them.

Gulliver was not anxious to stay in Balnibarbi, and he soon found that he could travel by ship to GLUBBDUB-DRIB. This was a fertile and picturesque island inhabited by sorcerers and magicians. The governor had a palace in the center of a large park which was surrounded by a stone wall, twenty feet high. Inside the wall were beautifully kept gardens and orchards, as well as enclosures for cattle. There seemed to be innumerable servants but whenever he passed one, Gulliver felt his flesh creep. He later discovered that these people were spirits of the dead. It was in the governor's power to call them up, and although he was not able to summon the same ghost more than once in three months, the population of the underworld was so large that he was never without sufficient help. The governor was most courteous to Gulliver and called up the spirits of Caesar, Aristotle and others to talk with him, but when he invited Gulliver to spend the night in his palace, Gulliver politely declined.

After his visit to Glubbdubdrib, Gulliver sailed to LUGG-NAGG, where he discovered that some of the inhabitants never died. The idea of living forever appealed to Gulliver until he learned that these people, known as the Struld-bruggs, grew old just like everyone else. After their first century they began to lose their teeth, their hair and a large part of their mental powers, so they were very miserable indeed.

On Gulliver's final voyage he set out as the captain of a ship. Once again he met with disaster because his sailors conspired against him and put him ashore in an unknown place, the LAND OF THE HOUYHNHNMS. If you say the name quickly and in the right tone, it sounds like the whinny of a horse, and that is just what the Houyhnhnms were, but they were by no means ordinary horses for they were wise and rational beings. Gulliver described them as "abounding in all excellencies." In the same country lived some very inferior creatures called Yahoos, who were like the most primitive members of the human race. They were unintelligent and served the Houyhnhnms as beasts of burden in return for food and shelter. The horses were not only superior to every creature on their island, but they seemed to Gulliver to be superior to the people of Europe. They had no word in their language for lie or falsehood, so when Gulliver described the wars that were going on at home, they could only reply, "You have said that which is not." They could not believe in war because their land was entirely free from crime, avarice and cruelty.

Classical   HADES

Hades was originally the name of the ruler of the Greek underworld. Later he came to be known as Pluto, and Hades was his subterranean kingdom. It was bordered by five rivers: Phlegethon, a river of liquid fire; Lethe, whose waters induced forgetfulness; Cocytus, along whose banks the unburied dead were required to wander for a hundred years; Acheron, the river of woe; and Styx, the river of gloom. Of these the Styx is the most familiar because several ancient poets have described the difficulties faced by the souls who must cross it in order to reach the gates of Hades. Charon, an unkempt old man, was the ferryman; but although the spirits were weightless, he could take only a few at each crossing so there were always crowds along the marshy banks. On very rare occasions a living person managed to visit Hades and almost sank the ferry when stepping on board. On the far side of the Styx the three-headed dog, Cerberus, guarded the gates. The dead were often buried with a honey cake to throw to the monster as they passed him.

In the earliest Greek myths Hades is not depicted as a

HADES

place of punishment, although eternal gloom and boredom would seem an evil fate to us. As time passed, however, the kingdom was thought of as divided, and souls were despatched to areas where they were punished or rewarded according to the way they had conducted their earthly lives. We find such a description in Virgil's *Aeneid*, written during the first century B.C. Many of Virgil's ideas were adopted by Dante about thirteen hundred years later. They are described under "Inferno."

HAMISTAKAN

Iranian

The early Iranians believed in a country called Hamistakan which was inhabited by the spirits of those whose sins were more or less balanced by the good deeds they had done on earth. They seemed to deserve neither reward nor punishment, so they were allowed to live without too much discomfort in their afterlives. They did suffer somewhat from changes in temperature, but no more than the people of this world who are exposed to extreme summer heat or winter cold. Moreover they had the hope of a better life at some indefinite point in time.

HAPPY HUNTING GROUND

American Indian

The term "Happy Hunting Ground" was originated by non-Indians to describe what they wrongly believed to be the Indian idea of life after death. The Indians themselves almost never mentioned hunting in this connection. Their afterworld is a quiet place during the day, but at night the spirits dance, play games and build fires. A chief is their leader and they live much as they did in their tribes. Many Indians locate the land of their dead on the far side of an ocean and sometimes, though not always, in the west. There are tales of living people going briefly to the afterworld to consult the spirit of a relative, and also occasional tales of a person dying temporarily and returning to life with a prophesy for his people.

SEE INFERNO **HELL**

HOBBITON-ACROSS-THE-WATER

J. R. R. Tolkien · English

In the northern land of *Eriador* is a county known simply as "The Shire." It contains a number of villages where Hobbits live, and probably the most important village is Hobbiton-Across-the-Water because the two most famous Hobbits, Bilbo and Frodo Baggins, had their hole in the hillside there. If it were not that some of the natives prefer to live in holes, Hobbiton might be described as a typical small English village with farms and cottages, a shop and a mill beside the river. Even those who live in holes on the terraced hillside have provided them with doors and windows, fireplaces and gardens, and furnished them comfortably. Hobbits are small people, smaller than dwarfs, and they are good-natured folk, fond of a quiet, peaceful life, but they can be brave as lions when the need arises.

In the Tolkien books—*The Hobbit* and the trilogy, *The Lord of the Rings* (1954–1956)—their exciting adventures and journeys away from Hobbiton are described, and maps show the exact location of the many places they visited.

HODMIMER'S FOREST

The Norse did not imagine the reign of their gods as something that would go on forever. Their myths described a time called Ragnorok when wars and devastation would destroy the world as well as Asgard and the kingdom of the giants. Surtr, the flame giant, would come forth from the southern land of fire, brandishing a sword that would send out showers of sparks as he led the other giants to fight the gods. The loosing of the powers of evil would cause the three cocks to sound the alarm—one in Valhalla, one in Midgard, and another in Niflheim. Then two huge wolves would appear and devour the sun and moon, and Surtr's fire would burn up all the world except for Hodmimir's forest. There Lif, the last woman, and Lifthraser, the last man, would seek refuge and sleep through the dreadful destruction. They would be nourished, even as they slept, by the dew falling on their lips from Yggdrasil, the enormous and immortal ash tree. Much later, when everything had become green again, this man and woman would waken and come forth to establish a new world of love and peace.

Teutonic

According to a thirteenth-century legend, the Horselborg was a mountain within which Venus—the Roman goddess of love—was said to live, at least during the middle ages. The legend tells how a German minnesinger named Tannhauser was passing the mountain when a beautiful lady appeared and beckoned to him. Tannhauser suspected that the lady was Venus, but he followed her nevertheless. She led him through a cavern into the heart of the mountain where she had palatial halls, richly furnished. Some have called it a land of magic, and there he spent seven years enjoying pagan revelry. Then because his conscience troubled him, he went on a pilgrimage to the pope and asked that his sins be forgiven. The pope told him that it was as impossible for Tannhauser's sins to be forgiven as it was for the pope's dry, old staff to burst into flower. The minnesinger sadly made his way back to Horselborg, but after three days the pope's staff suddenly burst into bloom. The pope sent someone in search of Tannhauser, but he was never found.

HORSELBORG OR HORSELBERG OR HORSEL

European

West of the southern tip of Ireland there was supposed to be a circular island which some called a place of eternal pleasure and feasting. For many years it even appeared on maps. It was said to be such a wonderful place that many explorers searched for it, and when Portugese adventurers thought they had found it, they named the coast they had reached Brazil.

As late as 1674 the island was described by a Captain

HY-BREASAIL OR HI BRASIL OR ISLE OF BRAZIL

Nisbet who claimed that he had landed there and that it was inhabited by gigantic black rabbits. In the center of the island was a castle where a magician lived. The captain brought back with him to Scotland some wretched men who had been, he said, prisoners of the magician. He did not bring back any of the enormous rabbits. Perhaps along with their change in size, they had acquired more violent dispositions.

HYPERBOREA   *Greek*

Hyperborea was the land at the back of the north wind. It was a place of everlasting spring and is supposed to have been located at the northernmost tip of the earth. It was inaccessible by land or sea, being separated from the lands to the south by lofty mountains. The inhabitants, who usually lived about a thousand years, wore crowns of golden bay leaves, and were always joyful, healthy and at peace with one another. They worshiped Apollo, the sun god. He had once visited Hyperborea and given a golden javelin to the wizard priest, Abaris. This javelin had the magical properties of a witch's broomstick, so the priest was able to sit on it and fly over the treetops. Though he made his home in Hyperborea, he frequently took long journeys. On one of them he visited Greece and by his magic ended a plague in Sparta.

INFERNO   *Dante Alighieri · Italian*

The poet Dante Alighieri, writing in the thirteenth century, has given us a vivid description of Hell, or the Inferno.

He saw it as an immense, inverted cone having nine concentric circles, one below the other. The highest and most comfortable level was for those who had committed no crime but, like Virgil, were born into a pagan world. Virgil was Dante's guide as they made their way slowly downward through the circles. He was able to point out a number of the sufferers and tell why they were being punished. The many categories of sinners were grouped together. The hypocrites, for example, were doomed to pace their circle forever, weighted down by hooded robes that were made of lead, but gilded on the outside so that they appeared dazzling. The punishments varied, becoming increasingly horrible as Dante descended from level to level. There were souls who struggled fruitlessly to climb out of the mire of a filthy bog. Others were bitten by the snakes they wrestled with, and in the pit of disease were the falsifiers. As might be expected, there was also a level of perpetual fire, but Dante realized that freezing could be as painful as burning. At the very lowest point was Lucifer himself, a gigantic devil, frozen up to his chest in an ice field. He was a three-headed monster and in each of his huge mouths he chewed a living man—one was Judas Iscariot, one was Brutus and one was Cassius. These must have been the three that thirteenth-century Dante considered the worst malefactors of all time.

Celtic and European

Many ancient tales had to do with the perils of the sea, but mariners were frequently endangered less by wind and waves, than by the charms of mermaids, sirens and other

ISLAND OF FAIR WOMEN

INFERNO

beautiful creatures. If they reached the shores of the Island of Fair Women, they were actually in danger of dying either of unrequited love or of starvation. No escape was possible, and although some lingered in their usual shape, others were changed into animals or birds by the goddess who ruled there.

ISLAND OF JOY

Celtic

The Irish are fond of merriment and so they conceived this island where laughter was often heard, a place of light and happy hearts. Bran, the giant who waded across the Irish Sea, once passed the Island of Joy, so it must have been thought to be between Wales and Ireland. It was also said to be a land where the people had no concept of time. Perhaps that contributed to their light-heartedness.

ISLANDS OF THE BLESSED

Classical and Celtic

Among the many islands believed to be located somewhere in the western ocean were those of the Blessed. No strong winds blew over them, only the gentlest sea breezes. They were lands of perfect happiness where the inhabitants led active, joyous lives, with horses to ride, checkers and other games to play, or the lyre if one preferred music. The balsam trees were fragrant there, and so were the magnificent rose gardens. These islands were first described by the Greeks as an afterworld not unlike the Elysian Fields, but they are also mentioned in old Celtic tales. St. Brendan, an Irish hero of the sixth century who seems to have covered most of the Atlantic on his famous voyage and once celebrated Mass on the back of a whale, visited the Islands of the Blessed. One of them was afterward known as St. Brendan's Isle. He described it as a place where there was no night, and said that it was located just this side of the gates of Paradise.

ISSLAND OR ISENLAND

Teutonic

According to ancient legend Issland is a fair island off the coast of Scandinavia. Its harbor and sandy beach are bordered by a wide plain where fairies sometimes hold their revels. Across the plain but within sight of the harbor rise the green turrets of the castle Isenstein. When Siegfried, the Teutonic hero, and his noble horse Greyfell landed on the island, the castle was surrounded by a moat of blazing fire. Flames leaped six or eight feet high, and Siegfried knew it was his task to ride through the fire to rescue Brunhild the princess, who with all her courtiers lay sleeping within those green stone walls. Only the power of his wonderful horse gave Siegfried the courage to go forward, but Greyfell cleared the fiery moat in a single leap. They found the gates wide open, the guards asleep at their posts, the dinner guests asleep at the banquet table, all waiting for Siegfried to break the spell.

JIGOKU

Japanese

Jigoku is a Japanese Inferno, an underground world made up of eight regions of fire and eight of ice. It is a kingdom ruled by a ferocious-looking creature called Emma-hoo. He is the judge of all the men whose souls pass before him. His equally savage sister judges the women. Emma-hoo sits between two decapitated heads from whom nothing can be hidden, and a huge mirror that reflects the past life of the soul coming up for judgment. The sinner is assigned to various regions of suffering according to the extent of his sins, but may be saved by the prayers of the living. In such a case the sinner may be reborn either on earth or in a happier afterworld.

JOTUNHEIM
ALSO KNOWN AS
UTGARD

Teutonic–Scandinavian

Jotunheim was supposed to have been situated on the outer rim of the earth. It was a dark and mountainous region, the home of the Jotuns—huge and powerful giants who were the enemies of the Teutonic gods. They probably personified the forces of nature.

KUEN-LUEN
OR KUN-LUN

Chinese

The Kuen-luen is a fabulous mountain located at the center of the earth's surface. On it grow the peach trees of life, and there, too, is the source of the Yellow River where the phoenix bathes. The ruler of this mountain is the Lady Queen of the West, Queen Mother Wang. She is the wife of the August Personage of Jade, and they live in a nine-story palace on the very top of the mountain. The palace is made of jade and all around it are the most beautiful gardens. It is a place of endless banquets and amusements, and the only human beings who ever reach it are those who are so virtuous that the gods permit them to eat the peach of immortality.

Bantu

Kuzimu is another of the many underground abodes of the dead, but the Bantu believe that it is also the source of earthquakes. From time to time there are mass movements of the ghosts which disturb the earth's surface.

KUZIMU

Chinese

Like many of the European peoples, the Chinese located their paradise in the west. They believed it to be very remote, separated from us by an infinity of worlds like our own. It was enclosed on all sides, but the spirits of the just who dwelt there were free to come and go among the other worlds, returning for their meals. Their lives were well-ordered and everything was controlled by divine law so there was no discontent or anxiety. The land had seven terraces, each with a row of trees whose branches were made of precious stones. When the wind stirred them they made delightful music. There were also lakes, crystal clear with lotus blossoms floating on the water, and beaches of golden sand. Birds with many-colored plumage lived in the land and their songs harmonized with the chiming trees and the happy voices of the spirits.

LAND OF
EXTREME FELICITY
IN THE WEST

LAND OF PROMISE

Celtic

In early Irish mythology there was said to be a country under the sea known as the Land of Promise, or sometimes the Land of Youth. In the center of this country was Connla's well and around it grew nine hazel trees. These trees were unusual in that they bore leaves, blossoms and nuts all at the same time, and the nuts were magical. Anyone who ate them acquired great knowledge and inspiration. The well was an extremely large one, both wide and deep, so salmon lived in its waters and when the hazelnuts fell in, the salmon ate them. Sometimes in fairy tales we read about a wise salmon speaking to a fisherman, and it is very likely a fish that has eaten a nut in the Land of Promise.

LANDS OF MONSTROUS PEOPLES

European and Asiatic

An ancient Chinese encyclopedia says that there are thirty-six lands beyond the seas, each one inhabited by people who are deformed or peculiar in appearance. Those who lived at *Jon-li*, for example, had only one hand and one foot. In another place there were giraffe-like people known as the Long-legs. In both the Chinese and the Greek legends a land is described where the inhabitants had only one eye, located in the middle of the forehead. Herodotus, the Greek historian, wrote about them and said they were cannibals. According to his tale they frequently bought young prisoners from other nations, herded them like cattle and fattened them up for dinner. Their land was never exactly located, though one early traveler and teller of tall tales, Aristeus, went so far as to place it on the banks of a river whose sands were pure gold. He called the inhabitants the toughest of all human beings and described them as hairy savages. Another traveler, Medasthenes, said that these people had ears like dogs and stiff bristles for hair. The one point everyone agreed on was the single eye. Some of these tales may have developed from the myth of the Cyclops, a race of brutal, one-eyed giants who were supposed to have lived on an island in the Mediterranean Sea.

Medasthenes may have been combining the myth of the one-eyed with the myth of the dog-headed people. According to the Chinese legend, these people have human bodies with the heads of dogs. The men are said to bark, but the women are able to speak. In Estonian and Latvian folktales the *Land of the Dog-heads* is at the end of the world. For the most part the inhabitants have the head of a dog, but some of them are divided vertically and have on the right side a human hand and foot, and on the left, two paws. They are said to attack and rob people who approach their borders.

Herodotus and another historian, Josephus, who lived in the first century A.D., go even further than this and describe a race of people in the vicinity of what is now Libya, who have no heads at all.

Rabelais · French   LANTERN-LAND

In his tales about the giant Pantagruel, which were published in 1532, the scholar and writer Rabelais tells about an island inhabited by the Lanternois. They are a

LANDS OF MONSTROUS PEOPLES

group of philosophers, writers and theologians who, although they are able to walk and speak, closely resemble lanterns. They do not look alike, however, for over the centuries lanterns have been made in many shapes and sizes. When dinner time comes in Lantern-Land each one is served a large new candle, and before long the company glows. Rabelais's intention was to ridicule those who pretended to more knowledge than they had.

LAPUTA SEE GULLIVER'S TRAVELS

LEMURIA *Geological and mythical*

Geologists have given the name Lemuria to a sunken continent which was thought to have connected India and Madagascar. There were many changes in the earth's surface in prehistoric times and even in later periods, and it is known that former bodies of land are now under water, but the speculations about the people of Lemuria would be hard to prove. Some said that they were twelve to fifteen feet tall and had flat faces. They also had enormous hands and feet, and a third eye in the backs of their heads so that they could walk as easily backwards as forwards. They dressed in robes of reptile skins and used wooden spears. Over the centuries the inhabitants were supposed to have grown more like the people of today, but they were never very intelligent. There are those who believe that Lemuria is beginning to rise again.

Classical LETHE

The river Lethe which bordered Hades has been called the river of oblivion. Those who drank from its waters forgot everything they had ever known.

SEE GULLIVER'S TRAVELS LILLIPUT

Lewis Carroll · English LOOKING-GLASS LAND

The map of Looking-Glass Land is neatly squared off like a huge chessboard which Alice has to travel across, following the moves of a pawn until she becomes a queen. This is the general plan of Lewis Carroll's book *Through the Looking-Glass and What Alice Found There*, but anyone who has ever tried to tie a bow or draw a diagram while watching a reflection in a mirror, knows how confusing a mirror-image can be. That is the way Alice found things in Looking-Glass Land, quite the opposite of what she might have expected. As the White Queen explained to her, "Living backwards always makes you a little giddy at first." The queen then proceeded to scream like a steam whistle because in a moment or two she was going to prick her already-bandaged finger. The countryside of the chessboard with its gardens and fields, its railway carriages and village shops, resembles England the way the right hand resembles the left—the same and yet so very different.

SEE GULLIVER'S TRAVELS LUGGNAGG

LYONESSE
ALSO CALLED LOGRIS
AND LUGDUNENSIS

Off the coast of Cornwall in England was once the land of Lyonnesse, where some of the stories in the King Arthur cycle are said to have taken place. It was a flourishing country in those days and one of its famous sons was Sir Tristram. The early English chronicles say that Lyonnesse was suddenly engulfed by the sea. Only one man escaped. His name was Trevillon and he leaped on his horse and rode madly toward Cornwall as the land behind him sank. Cornish fisherman have said that on nights when the sea is unusually clear, they have seen the turrets of castles beneath the waves. No one has ever discovered anything to prove that their stories are true, but Cornishmen have magic eyes and have been known to see mermaids and piskies.

MAG MEL

Celtic

Mag Mel was a delightful plain not unlike the Elysian Fields, where the souls of the dead found happiness. It is described in Irish folklore as a place of continuous feasting and pleasure. No one was ever required to work there.

MAG MOR

Celtic

Mag Mor was a land of the gods where there was always music in the air. It was a magic country where people were invisible but were able to see and appreciate the beauty around them. They never suffered the aches and pains of old age, nor was there any jealousy or disagreement among them. Everything was in abundance, but there was no private ownership, which would probably have been difficult to enforce anyway if one's neighbors were invisible.

Various mythologies

Claudius Ptolomy, an Alexandrian astronomer and geographer who lived in the second century A.D., was one of those who described magnetic islands. He said these islands contained a lodestone mountain with so powerful an attraction that it could pull a ship toward it if the ship had been built with iron nails. Such islands are also described in the *Arabian Nights* and in the *Travels of Sir John Mandeville*, a fourteenth-century author who located them in Asia.

Celtic

Maildun was an Irish hero who traveled with his companions in a curraugh, a long canoe made of a light wooden framework covered with the skins of animals. His voyage out into the Atlantic lasted three years and seven months, and he visited more than thirty islands. Most of them are interesting only because of the curious creatures or people inhabiting them. The island of red-hot animals, for example, was populated by herds of bright-red animals resembling small pigs. Their color was due to the fact that they were actually glowing like hot coals. Only one island was given a specific name, *Encos*, which means "one foot." Maildun and his men were unable to land there because it stood so high above the water they could find no way of climbing up, and they could see that it was supported underneath by a central pillar that rose from the depths of the sea.

MAGNETIC ISLANDS

The most interesting island was that of the mystic lake. On one side it was heavily wooded with old oaks and yew trees, and on the other it was a grassy plain where flocks of sheep were grazing, but in the middle was a tiny lake with a rocky hillock beside it. One morning Maildun and his men saw an enormous black bird land on the hillock. In its talons it carried a branch as big as a tree, covered with cherry-like fruits. At first the men were terrified by the size of the bird, but as they continued looking at it, they realized that it was very old and bedraggled. Its eyes were so dim it hardly seemed to see them at all. Before long two other birds appeared, equally large, but in much better condition. They began to groom the old bird, pulling out the dead feathers and preening the others. From time to time all three of them ate the fruits from the branch and dropped the pits into the lake. When the grooming was finished, the old bird bathed in the lake, and then helped his attendants arrange his feathers. As he did this, Maildun noticed that he was no longer old. His eyes were bright and his actions quick. Soon he spread his wings and flew off with his companions. Maildun's men were afraid to touch the magic waters of the little lake, but he himself bathed in it and felt wonderfully invigorated.

MALE AND FEMALE ISLANDS

Marco Polo · Italian

Marco Polo, who traveled during the thirteenth century, sometimes described lands he had heard of but not actually visited. Among these places were two islands located about five hundred miles south of India. They were called Male and Female because one was inhabited entirely by men, and the other by women and children. Every spring the men loaded their boats with rice and barrels of salted fish and set out to make the thirty-mile journey to the other island. After their arrival they tilled the soil and planted crops for the women. Three months later they departed, taking with them all the boys over the age of twelve. The women did the harvesting and also picked fruit from a variety of trees. The climate of these islands was mild and everyone led simple, contented lives.

Rabelais·French   MEDAMOTHY

Pantagruel, the gigantic hero of one of Rabelais's books, set sail with a fleet of ships to visit an oracle. He made his first stop at an island called Medamothy, a name derived from the Greek word for nowhere. Like many travelers he was interested chiefly in the colorful markets at the port where he and his friends made some unusual purchases. Perhaps the strangest was an animal. It was called the tarand, a creature about the size of a bullock with a head like a stag and enormous antlers. It was covered with long hair like a bear and its skin was as hard as steel. But the strangest thing was its ability to change color like a chameleon. When it stood near Pantagruel's scarlet cloak, its shaggy coat soon matched it, but when it walked beside the bushes, its hair became green.

Teutonic–Scandinavian   SEE ALSO GINNUNGAGAP   MIDGARD

Midgard is the name given to the earth in northern mythology. It was made from the body of the giant Ymir. The gods made land from his flesh, mountains from his bones, and trees from his hair. They raised his huge skull on pillars and that became the vault of the heavens in which they placed the sun, moon and stars. According to one myth people came from the vegetable kingdom. The gods gave the powers of motion and reason to two trees. The man was called Ask or Ash and the woman, Embia. The gods also took grubs and made them into one group of dwarfs who were compelled to live underground.

MIRKWOOD   SEE ALSO HOBBITON   *Tolkien · English*

There was no way for Bilbo Baggins, the Hobbit, and his dwarf companions to avoid going through Mirkwood unless they were willing to walk six hundred miles around it, so— frightening as it was—they took the forest path. It was a dark, gloomy place, and so silent that the very trees seemed to be listening. Worst of all it was inhabited by gigantic spiders that spun heavy, sticky webs and considered that a dwarf or a hobbit made a delicious meal. There were also wood elves living in the forest, who would have been good fellows if they had not been so eager to amass treasure.

MO   *L. Frank Baum · American*

In *The Magical Monarch of Mo*, Baum describes a kingdom where anyone could find food for the taking. Snow in that country was buttered popcorn. There was a river of milk with cheese islands where the natives dug all the cheese they could use. There were also trees that produced useful fruits such as boots and shoes, or even knives and swords.

MORDOR

Tolkien · English   SEE ALSO HOBBITON

Mordor was a shadowy land where so much evil dwelt that a smog always hung over it. It was surrounded by rugged mountains with such sharp, rocky faces that it was almost impossible to climb over them, and huge ogre-like orcs were on guard to capture or kill anyone who tried. In the center of the country was a wide plateau overlooked by the dark tower. That was the home of the dark lord Sauron, who sought the power to overthrow all the good forces in the world. In Mordor, too, was Mount Doom, a volcano having near its peak the Crack of Doom. Frodo, the Hobbit, had the dreadful if not impossible task of journeying into this land to throw Sauron's ring of power into the Crack of Doom where eternal fires would consume it.

MOUNT MASHU

SEE ERIDU

MOUNT MERU

Indian

Some of the peoples of ancient India thought that the earth was round, but flat—not a globe but a disk. In the center of it was Mount Meru. Indra, one of the chief gods and wielder of the thunderbolt, lived on top of the mountain. He was therefore not only in the center of the earth but halfway between earth and heaven.

MU

Speculative

The enormous statues and archeological mysteries found on Easter Island and on various other groups of islands have caused people to speculate about the possibility of a sunken continent in the Pacific Ocean. The continent has been given the name of Mu. It is thought to have been very extensive, including the Fiji and Hawaiian Islands, as well as Easter Island and the Marianas. Much of the description of the land is based on psychic intuition. It is said to have had a population of some sixty-four million people who were divided into ten tribes and ruled by a priest-emperor. It was a flat country covered with tropical vegetation, but with many buildings and a high degree of civilization. At the time of its existence there were no mountains on the earth. Then, about 13,000 years ago, huge underground caves of gas suddenly collapsed lowering Mu beneath the sea, except for the groups of islands. At the same time mountains arose on other continents.

MUSPELHEIM SEE GINNUNGAGAP

NAI THOMBO THOMBO

Fijian

Many myths about an afterworld describe it as a terribly difficult place for a soul to reach. Arrival at Nai Thombo Thombo is well-nigh impossible, and unmarried people have no chance whatever of getting there. The male soul sets out along a path and his first task is to hurl a whale's tooth at a particular tree. If he misses, he has to go back, but if he hits the tree he moves on to a waiting place where he stays until the souls of his wives catch up with him. Then they go on together, fighting demons every step of the way. If the demons win, they eat the souls. If the souls win, they continue until they come to a mountain where the husband is questioned about his former life. Then he may be sent back for reincarnation on earth, or thrown into the sea which is the last stage of the journey. When he, and presumably his wives as well, are washed ashore in Nai Thombo Thombo, they find life there quite similar to that on earth. Fijians believe they know the actual road a soul first has to follow. It runs through some of their villages so they are careful to keep it clear of anything that might hurt the spirits or trip them up.

C. S. Lewis · English   NARNIA

Narnia, the magical land created by C. S. Lewis, could sometimes be reached through an opening behind some old fur coats that hung in a wardrobe. Then again it might be beyond the laurel bushes in back of a school, or you might quite suddenly be dragged there from the waiting room of a railway station. It was a fairly large country according to Mr. Tumnis, the faun who had always lived there. It included all the land that lay between the lamppost and the great castle of Cair Paravel on the Eastern Sea, and the wild woods of the west. It was a land of crisp snowy winters and warm, bright summers. But the most fascinating thing about it were the creatures who lived in its forests, burrows and castles. There were centaurs, dwarfs and witches, badgers, wolves and English-speaking beavers, and, of course, the wonderful lion, Aslan. The way there is described in *The Lion, the Witch and the Wardrobe, The Magician's Nephew* and several other books by the same author.

NARNIA

NENOKATATSU-KUNI
OR NENO-KUNI
OR YOMOTSU-KUNI

Japanese

In Japanese mythology we are told that the land of night—which is also called the land of the dead and the land of roots—can be reached in two ways. There is a sloping and twisting lane that starts in the Izumo province of southeastern Japan. It winds its way downhill into the subterranean region where palaces and cottages are to be found. The other route is by way of the seashore, and leads into a bottomless abyss. Very little description of the country has been handed down in ancient tales, but demons, both men and women, dwell there. The women are known as the ugly ones, or the frowning ones.

Two of the earliest Japanese gods, who were parents of many gods and goddesses, were Izanami and his wife, Izanagi. When Izanagi died—for although they were gods they seem not to have been immortal—her husband could not bear to be without her. He made his way down into Neno-Kuni and found his wife there. When he asked her to go back with him, she said she thought she could not because she had eaten food after her arrival in the lower world. This tale bears an interesting resemblance to the Greek myth about Proserpine, but the ending is quite different. Izanagi tells her husband she will enter one of the buildings to find out whether it is possible for her to return to earth, but he must on no account follow her. He disobeys and in her wrath, she sends the evil women-demons to drive him away, and he never sees her again.

NEPHELOCOCCYGLA
OR CLOUD-CUCKOO-LAND

Aristophanes · Greek

In his famous comedy *The Birds*, which was first produced about 414 B.C., Aristophanes describes a city built by vast numbers of birds. It was located in the sky, halfway between heaven and earth. No character explains how the place was supported in midair, but if it was by clouds as the name suggests, they must have been unusually substantial because the city was surrounded by a high wall. The idea of building such a place was to make the birds the supreme rulers of heaven and earth. They could intercept incense and the odors of sacrifice rising from men to gods, and could stop any attempt of the gods to descend to earth. But the birds were not quite so intelligent as they thought they were, and the plan failed to work. Aristophanes was satirizing the Athenians, who at that time were waging wars to gain more power and wealth. He saw them as seeking to become gods, trying to put on wings and rule the world. He suggests that since they cannot achieve this ambition, their future will be one of unhappiness and discontent.

J. M. Barrie · Scottish

NEVERLAND OR NEVER-NEVER-LAND

A map of the Neverland can be found in every child's mind, and it is always more or less an island. It has zigzag roads and coral reefs and caves through which a river runs. But the map is confusing to read because everything keeps going around. Of course the place is inhabited. There are pirates and Indians, gnomes and fairies, lost boys (because the girls are too smart to get lost) and Peter Pan, the child who never grew up. The map would help you to recognize the country if you ever got there, but getting there is the problem. The best directions Peter could give were "second to the right and straight on till morning."

NEW ATLANTIS SEE BENSALEM

NIEBELUNGENLAND

Teutonic

The Niebelungenland cannot be located. It was probably
in the north, but beyond any horizon the human eye can
see. It was a place of mountains and valleys, fogs and thick
vapors. Elves and fairies peered out of its rocky crevices.
On one steep mountainside Siegfried, the Teutonic hero,
found two young princes starving because they could not
bear either to leave or to divide the heaps of gold and
precious stones lying between them. Siegfried made the
division but he was too late. The princes were so weak
they were unable to rise and soon died, lying upon their
piles of treasure. Many were Siegfried's adventures in this
land before its inhabitants swore fealty to him as their
prince.

NIFLHEIM

Teutonic–Scandinavian

The Scandinavian underworld of Niflheim was cold and
damp, and twelve poisonous rivers flowed out of it. It was
divided into nine kingdoms where giants lived, as well
as dwarfs and the souls of the dead. The latter were ruled
by a goddess named Hel whose gates, like those of Hades,
were guarded by a monstrous dog. The dog prevented any
mortal from entering the land. Firmly rooted in Niflheim
was the enormous and eternal ash tree called Yggdrasil.
Its huge trunk rose through the earth and its branches

reached the sky, where the horse of the chief god, Odin, nibbled its foliage. On the topmost bough was a golden cock whose duty it was to crow a warning to the gods in case their enemies, the giants, seemed to be preparing to attack.

This description of Niflheim places it underground, as it was in the later mythology. In the first creation myths it was located in the far north.

James Harrington · English — OCEANA

In 1656 James Harrington described his utopia, Oceana, in order to present his ideas about good government. He imagined a state where the prince, or archon, and all the other officials were elected to office. The citizens of Oceana lived in freedom and equality. The ownership of land was limited so that no one person or group could become powerful enough to dominate the others. In addition to the archon there was a senate to propose, discuss and enact laws, and a group of magistrates to see that the laws were obeyed. Unlike the creators of some utopias, Harrington did not conceive of a completely virtuous or altruistic population, but there was one point on which the Oceanians were unanimous, and that was their hatred of war.

Greek — OGYGIA

On his long voyage home from Troy, Odysseus's ship was wrecked, and he floated on one of the timbers to the island of Ogygia. This was the home of Calypso, who was one of the daughters of Atlas and had some supernatural power. Her enormous cavern was sheltered by thickets of alder, black poplar and cypress—trees of immortality whose branches sheltered horned owls, falcons and crows. Calypso held Odysseus prisoner for seven years and tried to make him forget his home in Ithaca, but she was unsuccessful. He spent his time sitting on the shore, gazing sadly out to sea. At last Zeus took pity on him and commanded Calypso to let him go, so she permitted Odysseus to build a raft and gave him food and drink for his journey.

OPHIR   *Hebrew*

Ophir is another of the lost countries which probably existed although it can no longer be located. It is mentioned in the Bible, always in connection with gold and precious stones. This is where King Solomon obtained the materials to ornament his temple. It seems to have been a long distance from Jerusalem because it took ships a long time to make the journey there. Some people think it was as remote as India or Ceylon.

OZ   *L. Frank Baum · American*

The land of Oz is divided into four parts, each originally ruled by a witch. When Dorothy's house was blown there by a Kansas cyclone, she found that the eastern section of Oz, where her house landed, was a beautiful country of trees, fields and flowers. She saw unusual birds there and still more unusual people. They were the Munchkins who, when full grown, were the size of young children. They dressed in blue and wore round hats with bells around the brims. Dorothy thought they were very pleasant and polite. They directed her to follow the yellow brick road to the center of the land of Oz where the Emerald City was located. That was the home of the wonderful wizard who could surely help her to return to Kansas. On every side of Oz was a wide desert so no one could leave except by magic. Dorothy's adventures are described in *The Wizard of Oz* and a series of other Oz books.

PANDEMONIUM

John Milton · English

When Milton wrote *Paradise Lost* in 1667, he described the capital of hell, Pandemonium. The council chamber of the evil spirits was to be found there, and the palace of Satan himself. Demons are far from quiet and orderly when they gather to compose their wicked plots, so the name of their city has come to mean noisy confusion or a wild tumult.

PARADISO

Dante Alighieri · Italian

The word Paradise was adopted from the Persian where it meant an enclosed park or garden, probably like a king's gardens with encircling walls. In this sense it has been used to refer to the Garden of Eden. It may also indicate a place where the souls of the dead wait for the day of judgment after which the righteous go on to heaven, or it may refer to heaven itself. That is Dante's conception. His Paradiso extends into the universe, and on his visit there he goes from planet to planet. He has no sense of rising, but as he moves onward he is aware of changes in the celestial light and harmony. He gives little background imagery because he is so overwhelmed by the love and wisdom and beauty emanating from those he meets.

PLANCTAE SEE SYMPLEGADES

PRYDAIN OR PRYDEIN   *Celtic*

Prydain is very much like Wales as Wales must have been many centuries ago when there were few towns and no highways. It has wild mountains and rugged hills with streams tumbling down to join the rivers, and its seacoast has both rocky coves and sandy beaches. Druids revere the oaks in Prydain's dark forests and gather beneath them to perform their magic rites. But there are open lands, too, with sunny fields and pastures for the sheep and horses. Bran, one of the giant-heroes of Wales, is said to have been a king of Prydain. He possessed a magic cauldron that had the power of restoring the dead to life, which must have been particularly useful to a warrior king.

Prydain has recently been used as the background of books by Lloyd Alexander.

PURGATORIO   *Dante Alighieri · Italian*

The poet Dante saw Purgatory as a high mountain rising beside the sea. The souls of the dead who had not been condemned to punishment in the Inferno arrived by boat to begin the long and perilous ascent. The mountain was so steep that they had to cling to the rock and avoid looking over the precipices on the outside of the narrow path. Those who had been proud on earth had to make the climb with heavy burdens on their backs. From time to time there were terraces around the mountain where the souls could rest and Dante noticed that, in spite of the hardships of the journey, he heard singing more often than the dreadful lamentations of the souls in the Inferno. Higher up there were steps cut in the rock and the climb became easier, but before reaching the top it was necessary to pass through a purifying fire whose flames cleansed the souls without consuming them.

Arabian

QAF or KAF or CAF

The Qaf is a mountain range made of emerald. In ancient times, when many people believed that the flat world was encircled by an ocean, the Arabians thought that beyond this ocean were high mountains that also encircled it. This range was the Qaf, and it was the home of the ginn and other remarkable beings.

Eskimo

QUDLIVUN

The Eskimos believe in a happy afterworld in the sky for certain groups of people. The first group are the kind-hearted souls who have fed the poor during their lives on earth. Next are those who have starved, and third, those

PURGATORIO

who have suffered or been miserable during their earthly existence. In Qudlivun they find compensation—plenty to eat and time to play games and to enjoy all the pleasures they may have missed.

QUIVIRA   SEE ALSO EL DORADO   *Latin American*

This is another of the legendary cities sought by Coronado and other Spanish explorers of the new world. It was said to be a place where fabulous quantities of gold and jewels were to be found.

REPUBLIC   *Plato · Greek*

In one of Plato's dialogues Socrates conducts a discussion on the concept of an ideal state. It is concluded that goodness, beauty and truth must be cultivated there, and that the government must be entrusted to only the finest people. Plato himself had made some attempt to enter political life in the Athens of the fourth century B.C., and had discovered that the situation was far from ideal. He was discouraged and disillusioned by the injustices he found. Perhaps for this reason he characterizes the leaders of his Republic as people of wisdom, justice, temperance and courage. Since the wisest and most moral would not necessarily be the choice of the majority of people, Plato's Republic is not a democracy.

SABBATICAL RIVER

Hebrew

There is an imaginary river described in Hebrew legends which takes its name from the Sabbath because on every seventh day it rested, and its waters remained perfectly still. In another version of the legend the river flowed only on the Sabbath.

ST. BRENDAN'S ISLAND

SEE ISLANDS OF THE BLESSED

SATIN

Rabelais · French

While Rabelais does not give much description of the places his giant prince, Pantagruel, visits on his voyage, the things he tells about the inhabitants are most unusual. In the land of Satin, for instance, there lived all sorts of mythical creatures including the hydra, the unicorn and the phoenix. There were also non-mythical creatures such as elephants who sat at tables to dine, to say nothing of being expert musicians and dancers. Many Greek gods and philosophers also lived in Satin.

SCHERIA

Greek

When the Greek hero Odysseus was nearly at the end of his voyage home from Troy, Poseidon, the god of the sea, sent a great storm that crushed the raft Odysseus was sailing. The waves washed him against the shore at Scheria where he managed to crawl up the beach away from the breakers. When his breath returned he struggled through the reeds along the shore and climbed a nearby hill planted with rows of olive trees. There he fell asleep and slept until he was wakened by the princess Nausica and her maidens. At first they were frightened to see a stranger on their island, but Odysseus spoke so courteously that Nausica led him through orchards of pomegranates, pear and fig trees to her father's palace. Alcinous, the king of Scheria, was also favorably impressed by the hero. He put him on board a magic ship that was able to take anyone to his destination in only a few hours. So Odysseus at last returned to Ithaca.

SCHILDA

German

Schilda was a mythical city whose inhabitants were noted for their great wisdom. They soon had such a reputation that people from every other town and country began to come to them for advice. This was a nuisance and the wise people, who were known as the Schildbergers, decided that the only way they could live in peace was to pretend to be stupid. They did all sorts of foolish things and took care that their actions should be known abroad. The plan worked perfectly and in a short time no one bothered them.

SCHLAURAFFENLAND

German

Somewhere to the west beyond the horizon is an island many people would enjoy. To enter, you had to eat your way through a wall of cake, and once inside you found a river of lemonade. Baked hams and broiled fish ran around the streets offering themselves to the inhabitants. At certain times it hailed biscuits or rained milk or soup, but one cannot help wondering what happened to the river when the soup came down on top of the lemonade. Some say this land was invented to make fun of those who were writing absurd and flowery descriptions of Paradise.

Japanese — SENKYO

This is an imaginary kingdom known in Japanese legends. It is a lovely mountainous region where the Sennins dwell. They are a people who are able to fly, walk on the waves and perform feats of magic. They can, for example, produce a horse from a magic gourd. They also enjoy solitude and like to commune with nature which they are always able to do amid their beautiful surroundings. They are a serene people who never worry or have any anxiety at all, and rejoice in living apart from the rest of the world.

James Hilton · English — SHANGRI-LA

Shangri-la is in the high mountains of Tibet, where a lamasery clings to the side of a cliff, its colored pavilions as delicate as flower petals. The snowy peaks of the Himalayas tower above, and below is the peaceful, fertile Valley of the Blue Moon, a place quite free from earthly cares. In Hilton's book, *Lost Horizon* (1933), two Englishmen, a woman missionary and an American criminal are transported to this remote spot in a hijacked plane. They discover that the Europeans and other outsiders in the lamasery live unusually long lives because of the rarefied air. The High Lama, a priest from Luxembourg who was born in 1680, lives until 1931, but any of these well-preserved people who leave the valley, quickly shrivel and grow very old.

SHEOL
Hebrew

The Hebrew abode of the dead was called Sheol, the land of forgetfulness. It was not originally considered a place of punishment, but in a later period it was identified with Gehenna, a synonym for Hell. There actually was a place near Jerusalem, where rubbish was continually being burned, that was called Gehenna.

STATES OF THE SUN AND MOON
Cyrano de Bergerac · French

Cyrano de Bergerac, the author who lived from 1619 to 1655, wrote Comic Histories of the States of the Moon and the Sun. These fantasies are interesting combinations of science, romance and satire, and are believed to have influenced both Swift and Voltaire. Cyrano describes constructing a machine propelled by rockets to take him to the moon. Instead of wearing a space suit, he coats his body with a quantity of beef marrow which is attracted to the moon as soon as he has left the earth's atmosphere. Upon arrival he is fortunate enough to fall into a tree of life. Otherwise, he says, "I should have been a thousand times dead." He discovers that the moon is like Paradise, with beautiful gardens and orchards, as well as inhabitants who have a very poor opinion of those who live on earth. Cyrano is first put in a cage and exhibited. Later be becomes a pet of the queen and is used to divert her and her ladies-in-waiting.

When he visits the sun, Cyrano is tried by a court of birds. The jury is lenient with him and the trial is really a condemnation of human nature. The birds are superior to people and consider them brutes who cruelly tyrannize over weaker animals.

STROPHADES

Greek

Long ago some of the Greek islands were thought to be not only floating, but also revolving. These were the Strophades or Turning Islands. They were sacred because they had been the abode of gods and goddesses, but their best-known inhabitants were the Harpies, bird monsters with human heads.

STYX

SEE HADES

SUKHAVATI

Buddhist

Sukhavati is a land of universal pleasure, peace and contentment. Its walls are made of precious stones and there are jewels on the shores of its lakes. The brooks and rivers are musical and as fragrant as the most delicate perfume.

STATES OF THE SUN AND MOON

SYMPLEGADES

In Greek mythology there are several references to enormous rocks that continually crash together and then spring apart. Sometimes they are called the *Cyanean Rocks* or the *Planctae* and sometimes, the *Symplegades*. In one tale the Argonauts were warned by Hermes, the messenger of the gods, that one of their greatest perils would be passing between these mist-shrouded rocks, which smashed any ships attempting to enter the Pontos or Black Sea. He advised the heroes to let loose a dove that would fly between the rocks. If the dove got through safely, the Argonauts were to row their hardest and they would be successful. They followed this advice and saw that only the tail feathers of the dove were caught, so they immediately started to row just as the rocks were pulling apart. As the dove had lost its tail feathers, they too had a little damage to the stern of their boat, but it was not serious enough to prevent them from continuing their journey. Their success broke the spell controlling the Symplegades, and from that time on, the rocks were motionless.

TALLSTORIA

Thomas More · English

One of the imaginary places described by Thomas More in the sixteenth century was a country in the east that he called by a Greek name that is the equivalent of Tallstoria. This remote land was far from the sea, and so surrounded by mountains that neighboring countries left it alone. The inhabitants lived happily on the products of the soil without either riches or serious poverty. If a thief was convicted there, he was required to give back what he had stolen or, if this was no longer available, to restore goods of equal value. He was then sentenced to hard labor, but not mistreated. He wore no chains and was fed decent meals, though he was not allowed any money or weapons during the time of his servitude. This concept was advanced and even considered radical in England at that time when thieves were sometimes hanged. More argued that if a man was starving, the threat of hanging was no deterrent to his trying to steal food.

John Mandeville · French   TAPROBANE

Among the many islands described in Sir John Mandeville's travel tales of the fourteenth century is one called Taprobane, which he locates in the eastern part of the Asiatic empire of the legendary Prester John. In ancient times Taprobane was the classical name of Ceylon, but the following details are all from Mandeville. He said it was a large and fruitful island surrounded by a shallow sea with water so clear that it was possible to see the sand on the bottom. The climate was mild, and there were two summers and two winters yearly so the inhabitants harvested their crops twice and always had plenty of food. They were governed by a king who was elected by the people. The most unusual thing about Taprobane was a breed of enormous ants as large as hounds. They lived upon a mountain of gold which they spent most of their time refining. Naturally the people coveted the gold, but the ants were vicious and no one dared go near them until it was discovered that in hot weather all the ants went underground at noon to cool off. Then the natives hastily drove their horses and camels up the mountain and loaded them as fast as they could.

TARSHISH

Hebrew

Like Ophir, Tarshish was a land of great wealth and commercial power. It is mentioned a number of times in the Bible, and probably existed. It was so remote that its fleet visited Palestine only once every three years carrying a cargo of gold, silver, ivory, apes and peacocks. It was on a ship bound for Tarshish—which one might call the end of the known earth—that Jonah tried to make his escape.

TARTARUS

Classical

A mortal visiting the Greek or Roman world of the dead would have to pass through Hades to reach Tartarus. In the *Iliad* it is said to be as far below Hades as the heavens are above the earth. It is a place of eternal punishment. Souls were first judged by Minos, one of the sons of Zeus, who condemned them according to their crimes. Sometimes the punishment was carried out by the Erinyes or Furies. These beings were not monsters, but women who might have been beautiful had not their faces been so fierce and determined. They were terrible, but they were just, and the punishments they enforced were varied. Sisyphus, for example, was compelled to exert all his strength in pushing a great rock up a steep hill, but when he neared the top, it invariably slipped and rolled back so he had to start again. Tantalus was punished by being eternally hungry and thirsty. He stood in water and sometimes it splashed as high as his chin, but he could never quite drink any. Beside him were trees laden with delicious, ripe fruit, but every time he reached out for one, a wind blew the branch just out of reach. Often the most severe punishments were meted out not to those we would call criminals, but to someone who had offended the gods.

Classical   TARTESSOS

Another of the lost lands people have tried to locate is Tartessos, which has been called a flourishing prehistoric sea kingdom. The Phoenicians, Phocians and others said that it was beyond Gibraltar, and so rich in silver that ships would return with silver anchors. It was said that Tartessos had commerce with Africa, where its merchants obtained ivory, and with the northern lands, probably Britain, where they obtained tin. One legend described waters coming up from the sea and engulfing Tartessos, and this led people to wonder whether it was part of Atlantis. Other tales have connected it with prehistoric Greece, because Tartessos was said to have had a king named Geryon, and one of the myths about Heracles tells of his stealing the cattle of Geryon in a remote land. Many scholars identify the Hebrew Tarshish with Tartessos, and place it somewhere on the coast of Spain.

Classical   THULE

Seneca, a Roman philosopher of the first century, called the island of Thule "the end of the earth." It was said to be in the far north where day and night each lasted for six months. The sea around it was supposed to be so thick that oars could not penetrate it. In the fourth century B.C. Pythias, the Greek navigator, said that he had visited Thule and that it was six-days' sail north of Britain. The term "Ultima Thule" was used by the Romans for the farthest point, and has come to mean some unattainable goal or even the end of the world.

TIR-FA-THONN   *Celtic*

Somewhere west of Ireland the sea is said to be so clear that as your boat sails over it, you can see the sand on the bottom, sparkling in the sunshine. The water becomes so transparent it seems as if your boat were floating on air, and then you can see a beautiful country with mansions and cottages, woods and fields. There may be people walking about or cattle grazing down there. It is said that this country, Tir-Fa-Thonn, was sunk at some remote time and is under an enchantment. If anyone could succeed in throwing fire on it, the spell would be broken and it would rise to the surface again.

TIR-NA-MBAN   *Celtic*

The literal meaning of Tir-Na-Mban is the Land of Women, although mortal men occasionally visited there. It was a fairy realm where everyone was beautiful. The food that was set before a visitor would taste like anything he wished it to be. But there was the usual fairy timelessness, with the disadvantage that upon leaving, the visitor might find himself suddenly wizened and old.

Finno–Ugrian   TUONELA

The Finnish land of the dead is dark and gloomy and, like similar places described in other folklore, it can only be reached by crossing a river. Some spirits go there by boat and others go over a bridge. The Finnish hero Vainamoinen, eager to learn ancient wisdom, went to Tuonela while he was still alive and had a difficult time returning to the upper world.

L. Frank Baum · American   TURVYLAND

In this country which Baum described in *The Magical Monarch of Mo*, everything was either upside down or backwards. The houses rested on their chimneys and the smoke went into the ground. The trees had their roots in the air. When people were happy, they cried, and when they were sad, they laughed. The creatures who lived in Turvyland were unusual, too. There were flying rabbits and skylarks that could never get off the ground.

Thomas More · English   UTOPIA

In 1516 Sir Thomas More devised the name Utopia from the Greek words meaning "not a place," and the book about his imaginary country became so famous that we now refer to any desirable society a person may conjure up as a utopia. More had an imaginary traveler describe what was in many ways an ideal country, and the ideas of its people and government were not only way in advance of his time, but some are still in advance of ours.

Utopia was a crescent-shaped island located somewhere in the Western Hemisphere. It had very few laws and they were so simply stated that the inhabitants could read and completely understand all of them. Therefore people involved in a lawsuit argued their own cases before the judge. Incidentally Thomas More was a lawyer.

In the towns of Utopia the houses were all the same size, and each had an equal amount of garden with flowers, fruit trees, grass and grape vines. Awards were given for the grounds most carefully kept. Though families lived in these private houses, they gathered in communal dining-rooms for meals, which were prepared by various groups of women in turn. There were fifty-four such towns with agricultural districts between. Everyone was required to spend at least two years in agricultural labor, but those who enjoyed it could make it a lifetime pursuit.

All people were educated to the fullest extent of their ability, and after mastering a trade or profession, they were required to work six hours a day. Another great improvement over the England of More's day were the spotless hospitals where the patients were so well treated that no one who was sick ever thought of remaining at home.

Clothing was simple, and adults wore no gold or jewelry. Such things were given to the children to play with, but mature persons were not supposed to want them. The Utopians had, in fact, more common sense than most of us have ever been able to acquire.

UTTARAKURUS
Indian

This mythical land, described in the *Ramayana* and *Mahabharada*, was a place where loving, happy people led lives of sheer delight. They were not immortal, but they never experienced ill health and they might live as long as a thousand or even eleven thousand years. At that point one might expect them to be more than ready to give up even the pleasantest of lives. The climate of their country was temperate, and the land was rich in minerals and precious stones. Perhaps the most curious thing about Uttarakurus was that trees provided for every need. They bore food, drink, clothing and ornaments.

Indian

VAITARANI

In Hindu mythology this is the river of death which flows between the land of the living and the kingdom of Yama, the land of the dead. It is a filthy stream full of loathsome debris. In order to cross it, the soul was required to grasp the tail of a cow. The same name, Vaitarani, is given to a section of the Hindu hell. This is an area reserved exclusively for those who were wicked enough on earth to destroy beehives or to pillage villages.

Teutonic–Scandinavian

VALHALLA

Odin, the chief god of Teutonic mythology, had three homes, one called Valhalla. There, in an enormous hall, he entertained heroes chosen from among the warriors who had died in battle. The hall was so big that it had more than five hundred doors, each of them wide enough to permit eight hundred people to march in abreast. Odin's guests, the heroes, were carried to Valhalla by the Val-

VALHALLA

kyries, awful and yet beautiful maidens who hovered over every battlefield. By the end of the day the warriors they had picked up had been healed of all their wounds and were able to go into the main hall to enjoy the banquet. One of the courses was a magic boar which obligingly came to life again as soon as all its flesh had been eaten. A she-goat provided a delicious mead for everyone to drink.

Outside Valhalla a fierce wolf stood guard, and overhead a mountain eagle soared to prevent intruders from entering. The castle was surrounded by a grove of trees with leaves of red-gold, and beyond the grove flowed the river Thund.

VOURUKASHA   *Iranian*

This is the mythical sea whose waters supply all the moisture in the world. In the midst of it grows the tree of life.

WAK WAK   *Arabian*

Bird Maidens came from Wak Wak, a land of Amazons. They were able to take off their wings and feathers at will and appear as beautiful girls. In the story, *Hasan of Bassorah*, Hasan married one of these maidens and hid her feathers, but one day she found them and flew away. Then Hasan had to make the long and dangerous journey to Wak Wak to bring her back again.

Lewis Carroll · English

WONDERLAND

One of the underworlds that is quite different from those of mythology is the Wonderland to which Alice descended in Lewis Carroll's book, published in 1865. Alice estimated her fall at four thousand miles, but since she was falling very slowly that is probably a great exaggeration. Falling slowly was just one of Alice's strange experiences. She found herself in a puzzling country where her surroundings were likely to change quite suddenly, or if they didn't change, *she* did. As she described it, "I'm never sure what I'm going to be from one minute to the next." But changes are interesting and so were Alice's adventures.

Oceanian

YALAING

Like most of the lands of the dead, Yalaing is a long way from our world. As they journey toward it, souls are provided with nourishment by two snakes forty miles long. They lie by the road, waiting to be eaten. Fortunately the diet is more varied and pleasing when the souls finally arrive at their destination. Yalaing has an abundance of game for the hunters, and good clean water.

Celtic

YS

In Breton legends it is said that the city of Ys once stood on the shore of the Bay of Trespasses. Its king, Gradlon, protected it from the sea and the dangerously high tides by building a great wall and a tidal basin to receive the overflow. This king had a wicked daughter who was very beautiful. One day she stole the keys of the sluice gates and opened them. As the waters rose, flooding the city, the king leaped on his horse and, taking his daughter behind him, attempted to reach the mainland. They were accompanied by one of the Celtic saints, Guenole. The saint, riding alongside, saw that the king's horse was foundering in the water, and warned him that his daughter was a witch and he could never escape while she rode with him. When the princess heard these words, she screamed and leaped into the waves. Her father reached shore safely, but the city disappeared forever. It is said that the princess became a mermaid and still haunts the area luring fishermen to their destruction. There are fisherfolk in Brittany who describe Ys as a city sleeping under the sea, and claim they can sometimes hear its bells ringing.